FIND YOUR VALUES

FIND YOURSELF

THE SIMPLE 3-STEP METHOD TO
DISCOVER YOUR VALUES AND BRING CLARITY
TO YOUR DECISION-MAKING

HANA WURZELOVA

Contents

Find Your Values in Half an Hour

You will find your values in the next 30 minutes with this simple guide.

Does it sound too quick? Too easy?

Well, it is actually possible. It cannot get any easier than this.

How can you do that?

As outlined in chapter 4, this book gives you a simple three-step method you can successfully use.

I have been using the method for years for myself and others, and it just works. The secret is keeping the process simple and focusing on one step at a time. You will have the results before you know it.

Know your values, know yourself.

The trick is not to overthink the whole process and not to end up stuck in philosophical questions. Just take the tiny steps, take action, and results will follow.

Tiny steps. One at a time.

This book will take you through actionable steps and show you lots of real-life examples from people in different life situations to give you a practical inspiration.

The journey will feel like an adventure where you will know more about yourself at the end.

First, you will pick personal values from a list easily. You'll find the most important ones following a simple method and finally give the values specific meaning.

At the end, you will have found your core values and gain more clarity and peace.

You will be able to go about your day and make better decisions, large and small, all because you are aware of what is important to you.

Find your values, find yourself.

Let the adventure begin.

CHAPTER 1

My Story: How I Found My Values and What Happened Next

Finding My Values for the First Time

How was my first experience with personal values? Life changing.

I was attending a weeklong professional motivational training in a beautiful hotel in the Austrian Alps. I was looking out the window as it was snowing. It was dark outside.

I was seated in a comfortable chair in a small library. I was right in the middle of exploring my personal values for the first time, holding a few cards with values written on them and thinking about my definition of a life well lived.

After some reflecting and soul searching, I eventually picked my top three values. Then we discussed our newfound core personal values in the group, in front of a huge fancy fireplace.

We had a beautiful, deep conversation when we listened to each other's stories about our biggest struggles, challenges, and dreams. It was almost magical.

I had no idea most of the magic was about to happen. By magic I mean big changes in our lives within a few months. A teammate had started her own business. Another teammate started a family and moved to a different country. As for me, I changed careers, moved outside of the metro area, and started a family.

A. Lot. Of. Change. Quite fast.

There were other colleagues who actually did not quit their job or move to Costa Rica. But from what I have seen, the people with the most disconnect from their values were the ones who made the biggest changes in their lives.

To be honest, I don't think just finding your values has the power to magically transform your life overnight. On the other hand, I do believe that it can be a powerful trigger for action.

The motivation comes from the misalignment of your values and your reality in life. Once there is enough motivation, the mismatch naturally leads to some kind of action.

As a first step, it is good just to be aware of the important things. Acting upon the knowledge is a natural result.

Other Ways to Find Values

Since that snowy retreat, I have searched for my personal values and myself several times with various strategies and results.

For a few weeks, I walked hundreds of miles across Spain following Camino de Santiago, a medieval Christian track. The experience was intense but also pretty challenging and took a lot of time and energy. Obviously. Imagine walking eight hours a day for weeks with no breaks. But it was a mystical adventure of a lifetime I absolutely loved.

Maybe if you have enough time and money, throw away this book and go walk the Camino in Spain. You will come back a different person.

Besides, I also took a bunch of online and offline personality tests and assessments of varying quality. They were mostly fast but also not as life changing. Even if I were able to find some of my values, I usually lacked deeper thinking about the everyday implications or real-life situations that would help me actually change my actions and habits.

This is why this book is as simple and practical as possible and gives a lot of specific examples.

Realizing what was important to me has always been an amazing and somewhat liberating experience.

For example, when I reconnected with my values, suddenly, I had a great and clear reason to say no to things I didn't want to do. It was clear they were not my priority. I had to make space for the important ones.

I felt I was not being selfish when saying no. I was authentic and focused.

Clear personal values brought more confidence, clarity, and harmony to my decision-making, both in my work and private life.

Others might have been surprised sometimes when I set my boundaries at work more clearly, for example, but eventually, they got used to the new situation.

I hope you will do the same soon. The method described in this book works magically even without fancy fireplaces and walking across countries.

Whatever your current situation, this book can help you bring more clarity into your life and your decision-making.

CHAPTER 2

What Are Personal Values?

Personal values are like a compass for decision-making. They state what your ideal behavior looks like.

At the end of the day, your core values define what you consider a life well lived. Values say who you are.

Imagine a person whose core values are Connection, Balance, and Honesty. Imagine another one with core values of Influence, Humor, and Happiness.

Can you see the difference between the two of them just from those few words?

One way to look at personal values is from the practical, day-to-day decision-making perspective. Then your values are the compass that helps you prioritize if you want to finish the project at work with stellar results and long overtime or you'd rather spend more time with your family this week, thinking your project should be just fine.

When you are clear about your values, you will also feel less guilty about whatever decision you make because you will know you live your values.

The other way to understand values is more philosophical. You can define who you are using values. You endlessly discover and rediscover your personality and aspirations. Then you can plan the big decisions in life and create this life well lived accordingly.

This could mean moving closer to your aging parents instead of working toward that promotion in a tech firm in San Francisco because you value connection over achievement. Or you might do the exact opposite. Both might be the right decisions for two different people.

Or you could postpone starting a family to make sure you are in a better position in your career because you value security over family in this case. Every person will have a different definition of what is right or wrong for them specifically.

What is your idea of a life well lived?

Why Are My Personal Values Important?

Every minute of every day, you choose how to spend your precious time and energy and where to direct your attention. Your time is the only nonrenewable resource you have available in your life. Money? You can always earn more of it. But if you waste your time, it will never come back. It is gone for good.

Right now, you are choosing to spend time reading this book. Just now you've spent a couple of seconds reading this paragraph, and you will never get those seconds back even if you want to.

The choice may or may not be conscious. You might not realize it, but constantly making the choice is what you do. What I do. What everyone does.

Your time is precious.

Knowing your core values can help you focus on what is important so that you spend your time well.

Your values define what success looks like for you. Society might throw their idea of success at you. Quite often, he who dies with the most toys wins. Quite often, it is "the person with the most cash when they die wins." I personally don't like that definition of success, but there are a lot of people who just buy into the race without giving it much thought. And then they end up feeling like something is off even when they reach all their sales goals.

You need to pay attention to what your own definition of success looks like to be able to create it. You need to pick a direction to be able to tell whether you've reached the finish line.

Your core personal values are like a compass. They show you the direction.

So here is the question: what are your core personal values?

Why Is It Important to Choose Core Values?

The point here is that in real life you need to prioritize. Let's get real.

If we could all live in harmony with all the values in the world, life would be easy. The reality is you can't prioritize everything at once. You need to choose what matters.

You go to college, travel around the world teaching English, or take care of your aging grandparent.

You can't go in all different directions at once. Too many compasses. Time is a limited resource, remember? You can only take one step at a time.

To be able to also live your values and not only write them on a pretty piece of paper, you need to find a few of the most important ones. Ideally, aim for three to five core values. And even then, you still will run into situations where you need to think hard about what is right for you.

Even those core values are most useful to you when prioritized. The order gives you clearer guidelines on how to make your decisions. When you decide your top value is Curiosity rather than Authenticity, then you will be more likely to explore new career choices when the situation presents itself. If it's the other way around, you'll probably just stay in your current job if you feel like it fits you pretty well.

Deciding what is the most important for you makes all the difference.

CHAPTER 3

Personal Values Examples

I love examples because they make you think more specifically and you can partially copy some of the ideas from other people. Make your life easy!

So let me share three stories with you. I believe that Amy the professional, Ben the student, and Cathy the stay-at-home parent will give you some inspiration and show you that finding your values is not rocket science.

Amy the Geeky Software Engineer

Amy is a software engineer. She is extremely smart, analytical, and introverted. She enjoys spending her days solving complex problems with advanced math, especially when her teammates already give up on finding a solution. She enjoys their good company and their geeky jokes.

In her personal life, Amy spends a lot of her time gaming and reading fantasy books. She lives in a spacious flat downtown and owns two cats. She enjoys occasional travel to remote places and mountains. She loves cooking with her friends when they have time. In general, Amy likes to have time for herself and recharge her mental batteries.

Amy follows the steps described in the method and finds that her top five personal values (in no specific order) are

- Competence
- Knowledge
- Learning
- Peace
- Security

When she pushes a bit further, she decides that her current top three are

- Competence
- Learning
- Peace

Amy feels better now as she starts reflecting on those core values when she feels like she has too much to do. She now stops for a moment and decides on what gives her the best value for her time invested.

She also managed to stop going to several stressful meetings at work to find more peace and to focus on the technical side of her job that she loves the most.

Ben the Curious Student

Ben is a hard-working college freshman who majors in psychology. He wants to give his best to his education, as he is passionate about what he has to learn. He likes exploring different theories and concepts.

Ben also wants to enjoy his college life to the fullest. He has a group of friends he loves to hang out with. They often travel together over the weekend for hiking or biking trips. As Ben moved across the country, he is excited to travel around his new home base.

In his free time, Ben works part time to cover the college tuition and fees. He lives in a dorm with other students, so he has study buddies available, and he likes binge-watching and the occasional parties.

Ben finds that his core five values are

- Adventure
- Courage
- Freedom
- Friendship
- Happiness

After giving his values a bit more thought, he picked his top three as

- Freedom
- Friendship
- Happiness

Ben is curious what will change in his actions after discovering his core values.

He tries to focus more on his top three values and feels like it is a bit of a struggle. It goes against his naturally carefree attitude. On the other hand, he notices he is more confident about his decisions when he takes the time to think them through.

His work enables him to be more independent and have more freedom, so working makes him feel better than traveling. He still spends time with his friends but tries to find a balance that works for him.

Cathy the Multitasking Parent

Cathy is a stay-at-home mom of a nine-month-old daughter. She originally thought she would come back to work sooner, but she decided to stay home for a few more months because of her daughter's sleep cycle. She also wanted to enjoy their time together.

Cathy used to be an athlete since high school until pregnancy. She had to take a break due to health issues. Now she is excited to spend time outside with her baby and occasionally go to the gym or for a jog. She still needs to carefully find balance between sleep and her workouts.

Cathy enjoys baking, playing board games, and philosophical discussions with her husband and friends. She found a group of parents with young children and spends time with some of them several times a week.

Cathy discovers that her top five values are

- Health
- Authenticity
- Harmony
- Love
- Meaningful Work

When she thinks a bit longer, she determines that her three core personal values are

- Health
- Harmony
- Meaningful Work

Cathy really values her health after her experience with having a baby, so she has already been paying attention to this in her life. She feels less guilty for taking time for herself after clearly defining her values.

She feels better equipped to ask for what she needs. She found a babysitter to give herself more time to exercise and takes turns with her husband to babysit at night to improve their sleep patterns. Cathy is getting better physically and mentally as well as a result.

What Are Your Values?

Now you have seen the examples above. Do any of the values resonate with you more than others? Do you seriously look at some value? How can someone have such a value?

The specific examples should give you an idea of what your list might look like and how to use it.

Now without further delay, let's go through the process and see which ones are the very best for you now.

CHAPTER 4

How to Find Your Top Three Personal Values

Let's start with the fun part: it's time to take action.

I recommend that you take a brief moment, sit down with a cup of your favorite coffee, tea, or hot chocolate. Possibly add your favorite music, a cool drink, or a warm blanket— whatever makes you feel comfortable.

Of course, you can pick your values without doing any of the above, but this way you will enjoy the process more and feel better throughout.

Take a moment for yourself when you can focus just on what you want and need without interruptions and with maximum comfort.

Ideally, grab a pen and a piece of paper. If you really cannot get a piece of paper, then you can type your values on a laptop or a phone. In any case, make sure you store the results safely. I love taking my notes and sending them to myself as an email so I can come back to them anytime on any device in the future.

If you have your favorite note-taking app, just use that, but make sure you will not lose the notes when you switch phones or uninstall the app.

The process is simple, so let's start and make it an enjoyable adventure.

Step 1: Pick 10 Personal Values from the Master List

The first step should take you just a couple of minutes. Go through the list of personal values I've assembled below. As you read through them, pick those that resonate the most. Do not think about it too much.

If you really feel like anything is missing, write that down.

If you struggle to get to 10 values, just go with seven or eight of them. The process will be even easier! Just make sure you have no more than 10.

If you have more than 10, just follow along, and things will get sorted out.

The Master List of 60 Personal Values

In my experience, there is no need for more than 60 values on the list. You can always add your own if you feel like you miss anything, or you can change the wording so that it fits your style.

Now pick your 10 personal values:

1. Authenticity
2. Achievement
3. Adventure
4. Authority
5. Balance
6. Beauty
7. Boldness
8. Compassion
9. Challenge
10. Commitment
11. Community
12. Competency
13. Connection
14. Contribution
15. Courage
16. Creativity
17. Curiosity
18. Determination
19. Fairness
20. Faith
21. Family
22. Freedom
23. Friendship
24. Fun

25. Happiness
26. Harmony
27. Health
28. Honesty
29. Humility
30. Humor
31. Influence
32. Integrity
33. Joy
34. Justice
35. Kindness
36. Knowledge
37. Leadership
38. Learning
39. Love
40. Loyalty
41. Meaningful Work
42. Openness
43. Optimism
44. Peace
45. Pleasure
46. Popularity
47. Religion
48. Reputation
49. Respect
50. Responsibility
51. Security
52. Self-respect
53. Service
54. Spirituality
55. Stability
56. Success
57. Status

58.   Trustworthiness
59.   Wealth
60.   Wisdom

Make sure you finish this step before reading further. It cannot be any easier than picking your values from a list. No deep philosophical reflections about defining life experiences or talking with your loved ones or therapists about what they think about you.

Just pick those values from the list now. It's easy. And quick.

Before you move on, stop and look at your shorter list now. Is there any value that you are sure you want to have there, and you didn't find it in the master list? Think for a moment and add it if you found one.

Done?

Good job! It was a piece of cake, right?

Now let's move on.

Step 2: Pick Your Core Values

You want to have three core values at the end. Making daily decisions based on them is much easier with three than 10 values.

A compass shows you one direction, not five or 15. How would you know where to go?

Drop the Least Important

When you look at your list, you may see a few values that you like, but you can tell they are not at the very top of your list.

Get rid of them.

The greatest enemy of great is good. Just drop the good values to make space for the great ones.

You're almost there now!

Group-Related Values

Your first step is to get down to a maximum of five values by grouping the values on your list into related topics.

You can group Love and Connection, for example.

You can put together Popularity, Status, and Influence.

I think you get the idea.

Now you take those groups one by one. You look at the values and pick one of them to represent the group as a whole.

There is no right or wrong way to do this. You decide what value fits you best. Everyone can have a different answer.

For example, starting with a group with Status, Popularity, and Influence, you could pick Influence because you want to inspire people around you. You see Status and Popularity as stepping stones for Influence.

On the other hand, I could pick Status because I value being an established authority and see Influence and Popularity as a side effect.

Think about your motivations and pick something. You cannot make a big mistake in this step.

Leave the values that don't fit into any group as they are.

Before moving on, pick an underlying value for each group. Ask yourself what is the value that matters most for you. Which one is the reason you've also picked the others?

Let's take the example of Love and Connection. What do both mean to you? Love may also include self-love, how you treat your loved ones, etc. Connection may mean a broader range of relationships with friends, family, colleagues, and clients. Which is important? Or is your definition different? You decide.

Another option to structure the values is to think about different areas of life. You can think about what drives you or bothers you at work, in relationships, and in your free time. Is there an underlying theme? A core value?

If you struggle here, you can make separate lists for work and private life, for example. I highly recommend having only one list, but you need to start somewhere and revisit and refine the list later.

Finished?

Great!

Find Your Core Values

After grouping and dropping values on your list, you may still have about five values.

In this step, you pick the core values.

This is the hardest part, so don't get discouraged. Give it a bit more thought.

Take your short list and pick those top three values by comparing one value with another.

You can write all values on little pieces of paper and put them in order.

Just compare them one by one, one values with another.

How do you do that? If you struggle, ask yourself these questions:

- How do I make big life decisions?
- How do I make small daily decisions? What is the reason I work at my job?
- What values do I want to think I hold? What are my ideals?
- What annoys me about other people's behavior?
- When do I feel like others lack a value that is important to me?

Take your time.

Are you finished? Good.

Congratulations! You've just found your top three values.

Give yourself a pat on back. You deserve it!

How do you feel? Do you have more clarity now?

Do you think you are better equipped to make decisions?

Take a moment and reflect.

You've completed the most important step of the process and already are in a much better place than at the beginning of the book.

Now what?

Let's look at how to work with your core values to get the most out of them. This is going to be fun!

Step 3: Craft a Definition of Your Personal Core Values

After doing the difficult work, you can have some creative fun with crafting a definition of your core values.

This will help you realize what your values mean to you.

You can incorporate more practical guidelines into the definition so that your values can really help your decision-making.

Unless you are able to apply your values into your daily life, they are pretty useless.

So how do you define your personal values? What do they mean in your daily life? When specifically are they reflected or violated by your actions?

Take your list of core values and write a sentence or two about each of them.

For example, if your value is Success, but you feel like the wording is not quite the thing you are looking for, just call it "Awesomeness" or anything that works for you and makes your heart sing.

Examples

For inspiration, look at other definitions of their core values.

Amy the software engineer described her values as

Competence. I work on being competent at work. I enjoy solving puzzles and getting work done. I like challenge and thrive when I can show my full abilities.

Learning. I keep learning to keep up with the newest technology at work, to understand the world around me, and to be able to create realistic opinions. I learn technology, languages, and random recipes and sports.

Peace. I make time for myself every day to relax. I resolve issues with others in a peaceful way. When I feel under pressure, I reflect and try to see how to proceed in a calm way to have the situation under control.

Ben the student defined his values as

Freedom. I am independent and responsible for myself and my decisions.

Friendship. I spend time with my friends on a daily basis, try to help them when I can, and enjoy our time together.

Happiness. I find time for the activities that make me happy on a regular basis.

Cathy the multitasking parent defined her values as

Health. I feel great in my body and can enjoy every day to the fullest. I sleep well, I eat healthy, and I try to limit stress when possible.

Harmony. I actively find creative ways to create harmony in my relationships. I feel harmony when I go about my day with my family and friends.

Meaningful Work. I see meaning in the work I do both at home and outside. When I know something is not meaningful to me, I try to delegate, cancel, or limit this activity. I look for new opportunities to create meaning even outside of my daily routine.

CHAPTER 5

What Do I Do with Those Values Now?

You go out and live happily ever after, living your values, and going through your life surrounded by singing unicorns and kittens. (Just joking.)

Almost.

Before you move on, it is a good idea to document your values so that you remember what you actually mean by them. Everyone's definition of success or reputation will be different.

Make Decisions Based on Your Values

Now you can benefit from knowing your values. Many people just run around the world making random decisions based on how they feel at the moment. You have a system now.

Do you wonder if you can commit to working for a non-profit you really like? Or do you need to make time for your health instead? Would you rather walk your dog than work? Would you go for a jog? Would you take an online course?

You have endless options for investing your time. Notice how you spend it and whether it is aligned with your values.

Aligning your decisions, actions, and habits with your values can be very powerful.

What's the pitfall? You may have to stop enabling others who probably want you to keep helping them, for instance. Just take your time, clearly communicate your motivation, and take small steps forward.

Do you need more time to sleep? Quit overworking at night. Try changing your schedule and find what works best for you and your job. It is important to try what works and be clear about what you want and need.

Your values are there to help you question whether your behavior and actions create the life you want to live.

Review Your Values Regularly

It is a good idea to review your list of core values either weekly or monthly. Build it into your planning routine or other ritual you have.

If you are a free spirit, then you can review your values when you feel they no longer fit your life.

For instance, you encounter a health problem and want to have Health as a core value now. Then add it to your list, write your definition for it, and prioritize against the other core values. Now you are good to go until next time.

It is natural for your values to change over the course of your life. There is a scientific psychological theory to it, but there's no need to go in depth now. You can always google it if you want more details.

I believe you probably have experienced a shift in values before. You realized you hated your job because you lacked a certain value. For example, more authenticity in client relationships.

Then you can think about whether Authenticity is your core value that needs more attention in your day-to-day life. Eventually, you might end up in a different role at your company or change your job completely.

We change and grow as people, and our values are a reflection of it. So no need to worry about finding the perfect values for the rest of your life.

Just as your values affect your life, your life experience also affects your values. It is useful to realize that and act accordingly.

Conclusion

Have you read through this book? If so, good job!

I hope you've taken action and found your core values. Most importantly, I hope they will help you make more authentic decisions and bring more clarity into your life.

You made great progress while reading this little book. You started learning about what your personal values are and how they can help you find clarity and meaning in your daily life, make the best decisions, and create the life you really want.

Finding your values can be a trigger for changes you want and need to make. Especially in times of change in your life or lifestyle, remember to reflect on what is really important for you. Take a moment and decide what you authentically want. With this knowledge, you can move forward in the right direction.

How was your experience with the method? What was your motivation at the beginning? Was the method easy to follow or sometimes challenging? Do you like the results?

Let me know your thoughts at hana@wurzelova.com. I will be happy to learn more about your experience.

Did you find the book helpful? If the answer is yes, please review the book to help spread the word and enable others to learn more about their values as well. It means a lot to me.

Thank you in advance!

Hana Wurzelova
wurzelova.com

About the Author

Hana Wurzelova is a nuclear scientist, top management consultant, and a nonfiction author. She is also a mother of two amazing daughters.

Hana has been pursuing many various passions—monitoring antimatter research, walking across Spain, driving from Europe to Mongolia, and managing giant international mergers—over the course of her life and enjoyed each of them in a different way.

Now she helps others follow their heart and live their lives to the fullest.

Printed in Great Britain
by Amazon

38975411R00030